This Blank Sheet Music

Belongs

To

Name ....

Email ....

"The beautiful thing about learning is nobody can take it away from you."

B. B. King

Title .... Date ....

Title .... Date ....

𝄢

T
A
B

𝄢

T
A
B

𝄢

T
A
B

𝄢

T
A
B

T
A
B

T
A
B

T
A
B

T
A
B

Title .... **Date** ....

T
A
B

T
A
B

T
A
B

T
A
B

Title .... Date ....

𝄢

T
A
B

𝄢

T
A
B

𝄢

T
A
B

𝄢

T
A
B

....

T
A
B

T
A
B

T
A
B

T
A
B

Title .... Date ....

T
A
B

T
A
B

T
A
B

T
A
B

Title .... Date ....

T
A
B

T
A
B

T
A
B

T
A
B

Title .... Date ....

T
A
B

T
A
B

T
A
B

T
A
B

Title ....   Date ....

Title .... Date ....

Title .... **Date** ....

T
A
B

T
A
B

T
A
B

T
A
B

Title .... Date ....

T
A
B

T
A
B

T
A
B

T
A
B

Title .... Date ....

Title .... Date ....

Title .... Date ....

Title .... Date ....

Title .... **Date** ....

T
A
B

T
A
B

T
A
B

T
A
B

Title .... Date ....

Title .... Date ....

....

T
A
B

T
A
B

T
A
B

T
A
B

Title .... Date ....

T
A
B

T
A
B

T
A
B

T
A
B

Title .... Date ....

Title .... Date ....

Title .... Date ....

T
A
B

T
A
B

T
A
B

T
A
B

....

T
A
B

T
A
B

T
A
B

T
A
B

.... Date ....

𝄢

T
A
B

𝄢

T
A
B

𝄢

T
A
B

𝄢

T
A
B

Title .... Date ....

Title .... Date ....

T
A
B

T
A
B

T
A
B

T
A
B

Title .... **Date** ....

T
A
B

T
A
B

T
A
B

T
A
B

T
A
B

T
A
B

T
A
B

T
A
B

Title .... **Date** ....

T
A
B

T
A
B

T
A
B

T
A
B

Title .... Date ....

T
A
B

T
A
B

T
A
B

T
A
B

Title .... Date ....

T
A
B

T
A
B

T
A
B

T
A
B

.... Date ....

Title .... Date ....

Title .... Date ....

Title .... Date ....

Title .... **Date** ....

Title .... Date ....

Title .... Date ....

Title ....   Date ....

Title .... Date ....

𝄢

T
A
B

𝄢

T
A
B

𝄢

T
A
B

𝄢

T
A
B

89

T
A
B

T
A
B

T
A
B

T
A
B

Title .... Date ....

Title .... Date ....

T
A
B

T
A
B

T
A
B

T
A
B

Title .... Date ....

T
A
B

T
A
B

T
A
B

T
A
B

T
A
B

T
A
B

T
A
B

T
A
B

T
A
B

T
A
B

T
A
B

T
A
B

T
A
B

T
A
B

T
A
B

T
A
B

T
A
B

T
A
B

T
A
B

T
A
B

Title .... **Date** ....

𝄢
T
A
B

𝄢
T
A
B

𝄢
T
A
B

𝄢
T
A
B

Title .... Date ....

T
A
B

T
A
B

T
A
B

T
A
B

T
A
B

T
A
B

T
A
B

T
A
B

Title .... Date ....

T
A
B

T
A
B

T
A
B

T
A
B

Title .... Date ....

T
A
B

T
A
B

T
A
B

T
A
B

Title .... Date ....

T
A
B

T
A
B

T
A
B

T
A
B

Title .... Date ....

T
A
B

T
A
B

T
A
B

T
A
B

Title .... Date ....

𝄢
T
A
B

𝄢
T
A
B

𝄢
T
A
B

𝄢
T
A
B

Title .... Date ....

T
A
B

T
A
B

T
A
B

T
A
B

Made in the USA
Monee, IL
26 February 2022

91940724R00070